ENGAGE!

To Create Super Performance and Profitability

ENGAGE!

To Create Super Performance and Profitability

Dr. Zayd Abdul-Karim

YouSpeakIt
PUBLISHING
The Easy Way
to Get Your Book
Done Right™

ISBN: 978-1-945446-67-2

*In gratitude to the Source of all life,
engagement, and happiness.*

PRAISE FOR *ENGAGE!*
TO CREATE SUPER PERFORMANCE AND PROFITABILITY

"This book will help you learn how to save on the high costs of disconnected and disengaged employees. As a result, improved interpersonal communication and processes will increase customer loyalty, productivity, and profits."

— Jill Lublin, International Speaker,
Master Publicity Strategist and Consultant,
and 4X Bestselling Author, JillLublin.com

"I endorse Super Performance."

— Berny Dorhmann, Founder, Chairman,
CEO Space International, Inc.

"Looking for ways to improve organizational health as a competitive advantage? If so, *Engage! To Create Super Performance and Profitability* is for you. It provides the blueprint for building a highly engaged workplace. It also offers a proven system for conducting an employee engagement program that produces results."

— Keith Leon S, Multiple International
Bestselling Author, Speaker, and Member
of the *Evolutionary Business Council*

Contents

Acknowledgments

In appreciation of my father, Lt. Colonel Louis E. Ridgley Sr. (1918–2015) and my mother, Mildred B. Ridgley (1917–2000), for all their love and sacrifices that provided me with opportunities for education and a better life. Appreciation to my wife Dr. Barbara Daaiyah Abdul-Karim, Lynne Rowe, B. Doyle Mitchell Jr., Ovetta Moore, Adam Markel, Keith and Maura Leon, Sunni Sukumar, and Nida.

Introduction

This book outlines a process for creating cultures of engagement and super performance in the workplace. Unfortunately, according to Gallup polls, seven out of ten employees are not engaged, or they are actively disengaged.[1] That means that they're not bringing passion, commitment, and extra effort to their work or to the organization.

Why does this happen?

Because they're not doing what they love, nor do they love what they're doing. Consequently, they may experience some degree of job misery, frustration, and emotional pain. When this becomes the reality of the work environment for individuals and teams, then it can spread throughout the organization like a disease. In some teams, it could be low level *dis*-ease, and in other groups it could be like a severe disease, such as a form of cancer.

By viewing the organization as a metaphoric body, you can see employee engagement as a critical aspect of organizational health. A person's body will not operate optimally when it is diseased. It becomes dysfunctional. The body and mind become weak and less productive. When too much pain sets in, the body becomes immobilized, deteriorates, and

---

1   "State of the American Workplace." Gallup, 2017. gallup.com/workplace/238085/state-american-workplace-report-2017.aspx

eventually dies. The same is true for an organization. In an organization, dis-ease leads to high costs of toxicity, turnover, absenteeism, preventable errors, and lower employee and customer loyalty. These conditions are expensive and limit profitability. This current generation of employees will leave a toxic work environment quickly because it's no fun.

I was recently watching the NBA summer league, and Isaiah Thomas—NBA Hall of Fame basketball player, NBA executive with the New York Knicks—was talking about this new generation of young players. He said they don't make decisions for the sake of money. They make decisions based on people they like to be around and based on whether they feel respected. They want to feel respected, they want good management, and they want a team of people they can trust to improve.

Thomas made the statement that younger players want to be emotionally happy because not being emotionally happy is hell in the workplace. I believe respect, trust of management, and emotional happiness relate to creating cultures of engagement. With this generation, it's part of their decision-making process. Any different environment is going to be toxic, and it will not promote individual, team, or business growth. Toxic environments create a reality of lack, less productivity and profitability.

What are the solutions to these negative conditions?

You need a step-by-step process so that you may:

- Collect reliable data
- Diagnose the organization's health
- Develop and implement a treatment plan
- Monitor progress
- Reassess the work environment

This book provides solutions to cure the dis-eases of team and organizational dysfunction, such as lack of trust, lack of accountability, and lack of teamwork and cooperation. It provides a road map for improving organizational health through creating cultures of engagement and super performance.

This book is written for leaders and managers who want to learn to create cultures of engagement in their work teams and organizations. I wrote it to share what I've learned about creating engagement at work and super performance, which leads to greater productivity and profitability. For me, this journey started decades ago when I was trying to find my niche in the business world. I bounced around to different jobs, not really clear about my purpose and how I wanted to contribute to society.

How This Work Started

I was thirty-two years old while studying for my master's degree at American University in Washington, D.C. Dr. Morley Segal introduced the class to experiential learning exercises. I fell in love with that type of learning and discovered my purpose for service as a trainer. Eventually, I decided to pursue a doctorate degree from Virginia Tech in Adult Continuing Education, specializing in Human Resource Development, Training, and Organizational Development.

Why?

Because I wanted more technical knowledge and experience in my chosen profession of training and development.

As I learned, I landed a few training gigs here and there and began teaching undergraduate courses in management. Eventually, I was hired as a trainer for a small consulting firm, Organizational Development (OD) Systems in Alexandria, Virginia. That work led me to a position as a corporate trainer in the worldwide management consulting firm, Booz Allen Hamilton. There I worked in the OD and training department teaching consulting skills, data-gathering skills, structured writing, and communication skills to consultants.

I stayed at Booz Allen Hamilton for four years, then bounced around to smaller firms consulting on projects with federal government agencies like the FAA (Federal Aviation Administration) and the Department of Labor, helping them to restructure the management/supervisory programs. Eventually I started my own business, Development Training Systems, LLC, and conducted needs assessments, leadership development training, team-building training, and strategic planning for teams and leaders. During that time, I taught graduate school courses at Johns Hopkins University in Leadership Development and the MBA programs.

I know this is a long story, but I'm trying to give you some context. My business did dry up after about ten years, and I took a job at Strayer University. Eventually, I was promoted to a senior management position as a Campus Dean, Chief Learning Officer. At first, I served 25 employees and 600 students. Things went well and they gave me two campuses, which meant 55 employees and 1,400 students. I served in this position for four years. Although I inherited disengaged employees and disengaged organizations, I was able to turn them around to become more functional. We hit our revenue targets and even won a few regional awards for leadership and team performance.

This employee engagement work began when I was in my seventh year at Strayer. They restructured the organization, and they did away with the campus dean positions. Some of us received a buy-out and others were repositioned. I stayed on for another year, teaching graduate courses online. I wasn't thrilled about teaching online courses full time with 150 different students every three months, but I was glad to have a job and health insurance. Eventually, after about a year or so, they downsized, and I was released as part of a reduction in force.

The interesting thing about that year as an online teacher is that I recognized my work could be turned into a business, and I named it Universal Self-Leadership Institute. One of my previous clients called me, and we became involved in employee engagement surveys. That's how all this started. I didn't know all my previous learning, training, teaching, and leadership experience would culminate in this type of work, but it did, and I love it. It's led to more opportunities to help people, teams, and organizations grow. In this book, I share what I've done with multiple organizations to help them create cultures of engagement. My intention is for you to receive useful benefits, insights, and tools to transform your team or organization to super performance with more profitability.

Major Life-Changing Event

Another reason for writing this book is that when I was at Strayer being promoted to senior management, I experienced a major life-changing event. There are approximately 115,000 people on the waiting lists for organ transplants.[2] The American Liver Foundation reports 8,000 transplants occur each year.[3] I was one of the 8,000 who received a liver transplant in 2011. I know the fear and pain of severe disease, living with liver cancer, and surviving a transplant. I know

---

2   "Get Informed," National Foundation for Transplants. transplants.org/get-informed/?gclid=EAIaIQobChMI1M-M8tjw3wIVCIRpCh00 cQs9EAAYAiAAEgISxfD_BwE
3   American Liver Foundation. liverfoundation.org/wp-content/uploads/2017/09/alf-poster-liver-transplant-jboike.pdf

the resilience of a two-year recovery period, with disciplined action, side effects, and progress to better health.

My journey back to physical health is a metaphor for regaining your organizational health. Those recovery experiences, coupled with being a senior manager who inherited disengaged workplace cultures from three different organizations, put me in the best position to teach what's in this book. By experiencing a return to *perfect* health, able to function fully in life, I became more productive and more profitable and have accomplished many things since then. I was given a new lease on life and wanted to produce something that showed my gratitude for life—something that lessened the learning curve for leaders and managers. I want to leave a legacy of transformational learning among my clients, friends, and all those who come in contact with this writing. I believe you will find it useful and beneficial in your professional and organizational growth and transformation.

Read this book all the way through, then go back to specific chapters that address whatever stages of the engagement process you're in, so that you can improve your organizational health.

I hope you receive insights, see a logical process for team and organizational development growth, and gain tools to apply to your current reality. Take baby steps forward to create a new reality, more consistent with the type of business and outcomes you really desire.

CHAPTER ONE

The Truth About Transformation

IDENTIFY THE ORGANIZATIONAL CHALLENGES

As the owner, leader or manager of a team or organization, success depends upon your ability to invest yourself wholeheartedly in the health of the business. Your buy-in is critical. Once you buy-in to supporting the health of your team or business as a whole, you are well on your way to creating lasting change that ensures success.

We all want the best possible existence in our businesses and lives, which means being actively engaged.

The Gallup organization's report, "State of the American Workplace," describes three types of employees at work:[4]

1. Those who are fully engaged and passionate (29 percent)

---

4   "State of the American Workplace." Gallup, 2017. gallup.com/workplace/238085/state-american-workplace-report-2017.aspx

2. Those who are not engaged—who are checked out and doing mediocre work (45 percent)

3. Those who are actively disengaged, unhappy, and in such pain and frustration that they want to infect everybody else (26 percent)

When you add the not engaged and the actively disengaged, 71 percent of employees are disengaged to some degree. Only three out of ten workers are really engaged. That's going to create organizational challenges. You must identify those challenges to address them; otherwise, you're just living with your *head in the sand*. That's why this is important. If you know better, you can do better and achieve better results.

Signs of Toxicity and Turnover

Culture is defined as *the way we do things*. Toxicity in the workplace is due to cultural breakdowns. Culture is extremely important in today's workplace. Employees have certain expectations of how they will work together. They want respect, good leadership, and a team they can trust. They want opportunities to contribute, learn, and grow. When the workplace culture does not meet their expectations, they leave. Toxicity leads to turnover.

Certain signs of toxicity become apparent, such as a lack of communication or a misalignment with strategic objectives. Toxic communication occurs when people don't trust each other and are unwilling to deal with conflict in healthy ways.

Misalignment results in less commitment and accountability, and fewer results.

I've seen clients disengaged for many reasons:

- There is a lack of transparency, secrecy or withholding information, politics, gossip, or insufficient communication.

- Culture of retribution or hostility, favoritism, or obsessive competition exists in the work environment.

- Teamwork is lacking.

- Policies and procedures are inconsistent.

- Senior leadership does not listen to the employees' needs and concerns.

- Mistakes are punished rather than treated as learning opportunities.

- There's a lack of accountability.

- People say things like: *People are looking out for their own department,* or *They don't keep employees' information and matters confidential.*

- Equality is not present.

- Employees feel disrespected.

- Management does not keep promises.

- Some members of the group look down on or label others as problems and push them aside.

All these signs are part of toxicity and will create a lot of problems within the workplace.

Ultimately, toxicity is going to cost money because poor attitudes lead to poor performance, and turnover will be expensive. The Society for Human Resource Management (SHRM) says that turnover can cost upward to twice the employee's annual salary to replace them.[5]

In one situation, a client lost $435,000 from a preventable mistake made by an employee known to be disengaged. They could not recoup that money. Additionally, that error led to turnover because the person had to be fired. Factor in the cost of twice their annual salary to replace them, and you can see the downward spiral of disengagement and turnover. This was a significant loss in profitability of over half a million dollars.

Check the Numbers

We're in business to serve customers and to earn a profit. You must pay attention to the numbers because they indicate when toxicity has taken over and is affecting the bottom line.

---

5   The Well: A financial wellness blog by the experts at Enrich. Enrich. enrich.org/blog/The-true-cost-of-employee-turnover-financial-wellness-enrich

In one company I worked with, there had been a consistent reduction in their operating revenue for twelve consecutive quarters. That was a major sign. Another client reported three years in which one unit did not reach their revenue goals.

Again, turnover is an outgrowth of toxicity. Identify your turnover rate, and you can calculate twice the average salary for replacing those employees. Check the numbers. *Forbes* magazine says that absenteeism costs an average of "$2,600 to $3,600 per employee per year."[6] Calculate how much that's costing you. There are further costs of misalignment with strategic direction. All this disengagement leads to deterioration and organizational death. Numbers can help you figure out the gap between where you are and where you want to be.

Trust What You See

You may involve yourself so deeply in the technical aspects of your business that you don't assess how to improve work processes. Remember, challenges are often about the dis-ease of disengagement; people are dissatisfied, unhappy, and in pain. These signs of toxicity—the turnover, productivity, and sales numbers going down—reveal that there is some dis-ease.

---

6   "The Causes and Costs of Absenteeism in the Workplace." Forbes. forbes.com/sites/investopedia/2013/07/10/the-causes-and-costs-of-absenteeism-in-the-workplace/#6112d683eb65

Think about an organization using the metaphor of a physical body. When your body doesn't feel well, you go to the doctor. The doctor runs some tests, gives you the results, and then creates a treatment plan to restore you to optimal health.

That's what this process of engaging to achieve super performance and profitability is all about.

First, identify the organizational challenges. This is like going to the doctor, discussing the test results, and checking out the data. You gather data because sometimes, your body is sicker than you think it is. Some diseases aren't even detectable unless you conduct certain tests.

Second, you must trust the data. If you find toxicity, turnover, cultural breakdowns, or sexual or other types of harassment, trust those signs that your organization needs to improve its health.

Third, begin doing the things that will help your organization heal. Pay attention to the signs, even though they may be painful.

We all are vulnerable to these challenges.

Yet, any high-performing organization expresses clear information in four different quadrants:

1. Cultures of engagement in which people feel empowered, challenged, and respected

2. Strategic alignment in which employees understand where the organization is going and how they fit in and will contribute

3. Motivation and relationships in which managers have positive relationships with employees and build cohesive teams

4. Managing execution in which expectations and goals are clear and people are held accountable

If any of these things are not happening, or if you don't have data to surmise whether these things are happening, challenges will persist and ultimately affect performance, productivity, and profitability. That's why we want to identify the organizational challenges.

ACCEPT THE PAIN

Most of us don't like pain. Some of us have a higher threshold for pain than others, but pain is something that we tend to resist. You can feel pain in your spiritual life, mental life, physical life, financial life, family, relationships, or in your own soul. When you sense pain, the natural tendency is to resist or ignore it, as if it's not happening. When that resistance becomes a habit, then you lose yourself and limit your possibilities for growth. The same is true within organizations.

The opposite of resistance is acceptance. You must accept pain as something necessary for your organization to learn and grow. There is a song that states that joy and pain are the opposite ends on the continuum of energy. We all want joy, but sometimes we must face the pain to experience the joy. They're both one and the same, two sides of the same coin. Both are necessary for the fullness of life and the fullness of growth personally, on teams, as well as in organizations.

Understand the Role of Discomfort

When we sense discomfort and pain, it's usually a sign that something is out of balance. Balance is the principle—in our lives and the universe—that's necessary for growth. If there's a severe dis-ease in the organization and an operation may be required, then there's going to be pain.

Let's say you require a surgery in which your abdominal muscles must be cut and the wall reconstructed. That pain, that discomfort, is a sign. First, something is out of balance and you need to regain balance. That's what leads you to the doctor for a diagnosis or surgery or treatment. Even in the process of recovering, that pain is a sign of healing. There are two parts. There's 1) the discomfort of what it is—a sign of something wrong—but it's also 2) a sign that healing is occurring once you begin the treatment and recovery.

This pain is really a blessing because it tells you what you don't want! Once you identify what you don't want, you can now figure out what you *do* want. The pain you feel calls forth a desire for growth, for reaching more potential—in life, in terms of evolving to excellence, and in human potential. In business, we measure in terms of performance and profitability. The role of pain is a benefit and a blessing when we can accept it and understand that it is leading us to better health and fuller productivity.

Look for the Mercy

I share this personal health experience in the hope that you will transfer the lessons to organizational health. I was blessed to be diagnosed with liver cancer years ago. There was really no pain that identified the illness. The only way to discover liver disease is through certain tests. When the results came in, it was a scary and painful report.

After I allowed myself to accept the shocking reality that I was very sick with a terminal disease, I began to educate myself. I learned there were options for me to grow and get better. It was either do nothing—they said I would die in eighteen months or so—or I could get a liver transplant. Now, some would think the liver transplant was a death sentence, but I realized the diagnosis was really a life sentence for me.

To date, it's been eight years since the transplant, and I've been able to produce and accomplish a lot of wonderful things, like write this book.

But I had to learn to ask: *Where is the mercy in this situation?*

These were some of the aspects of mercy I experienced:

- Physicians identified the cancer early enough for treatment.

- I received procedures that kept me alive long enough to get a liver.

- I was healthy enough to qualify for the transplant.

- The Almighty gave me a donor liver that was good.

- I survived the major, major surgery.

- I had insurance to cover the operation and recovery costs.

- I received ongoing treatment to correct intense complications from the side effects of medications.

We can think of organizational health the same way. What occurred in my body is just one example. I'm sure you know stories and examples of your own challenges or those of loved ones. It's the same as considering the health of a team or an organization. If you feel that pain and you search for the mercy in it, you'll find it.

What's the other option?

To think and feel negative about all of it by asking: *Why me?* which cannot be answered. Or by punishing yourself and feeling judgmental and hatred toward yourself and others.

Those negative energies are *not* going to create a solution; they're just going to create more of the same problems. So, when you look for the mercy despite the pain, I guarantee you will see the mercy. We accomplish what we strive for, and we need to learn how to recognize what's in front of us. Look for the mercy. Look for the good.

Everything in life is a mercy. The good, the bad, the ugly, the desirable, the undesirable; they are all mercies. In hard times and good times, you'll see it. Focusing on that energy and sending mercy energy out will bring more of it to you and more things to be grateful for. This works in business as well as life because mercy is one of the highest frequencies of love energy. Love permeates everything in life and is definitely required in business. We must love our people to help them feel valued and help them grow. We must love our customers and the service we give them. We must love our lives to live them to the fullest.

SHIFT THE MINDSET

When I started my business seventeen years ago, I learned a formula for transformation, a formula for improving results. The main factor in improving results is *positive behavior change*. If you don't change your behavior in the direction of the results you want, you're not going to improve your results, increase your business, and better your life.

Change is something that most people don't want. We see change as loss. We resist change. We're afraid of change. We need a process that's going to allow us to do what we usually don't want to do.

There are four elements that change behavior positively:

1. *Attitude* or shifting the mindset (the habits of thoughts and feelings that drive our behaviors)

2. *Skill* or knowing how to do something

3. *Knowledge* or knowing what to do next

4. *Goals* that are specific and measurable

Now, most of us have enough knowledge and skills to be on the team. Also, we've been conditioned to think that knowledge and skills are the be-all and end-all. They play their roles. But, I've found it's not a lack of knowledge and skills that keeps us from changing our behaviors and improving results. We've got the internet—one press of a button on a computer and you can access more knowledge than you can assimilate in a lifetime. That's not the problem.

The issue is our mindset, our attitudes (how we feel), and then whether we are clear about the goals and the direction in which we are headed. I've learned by helping people address their mindset and goals that they can change their behaviors and improve their results positively.

When I say *mindset*, I'm really talking about moving away from the negative feelings and thoughts. Let's go back to toxicity: that's when people complain, blame others, live as victims, gossip, or judge others. When people engage regularly in those feelings and behaviors, they'll attract more of the same negative energy. These are signs of disengagement, which detract from super performance and profitability.

We need to shift from:

- Selfishness *to* Selfless Service
- Frustration *to* Patience
- Powerlessness *to* Hopefulness
- Punishment *to* Forgiveness
- Judgment *to* Mercy
- Competition *to* Cooperation

Ultimately, we need to turn from hatred toward a mindset of love—all the different faces of love.

What's love got to do with business?

In reality, *everything!* Leaders who succeed are the ones who extend love to their people by helping them develop and grow, and thereby gain the love of their people in return.

The negativity of our dis-eased ego is what brings us down, but when we can come from a love-based, higher-principled, I'll even say *spirit-based* energy, we find that life does work a lot better. Love is the highest form of engagement. This may be intangible, or abstract, but it definitely affects performance and the bottom line.

Whatever energy you put out will come back to you. It all starts within your heart, within your mindset, within your feelings and thoughts. Change those habits and behaviors, and you'll change your results.

Pain is a natural part of life, and we are required to experience it to appreciate the joy that we all want. Remember that pain is temporary. There is an ebb and flow to life.

There's an old saying: *This, too, shall pass.*

When pain comes, know it will pass and lead to joy. When joy comes, know that's going to pass too, and there will be pain again. That's what gives us balance in life.

DECIDE TO TRANSFORM

A firm decision is a key to freedom. When we decide to do something, that means we must cut off other options. I can remember my transformation started when I was in college. I almost flunked out of the Pennsylvania State University because I was totally disengaged in life. My report card was a 2.0.

Have you ever faced failure, searched your soul, and made a decision to change?

I have. I believe most people have at some time in life. In that situation, I decided to change my attitude and mindset and set a new goal. I decided that I wanted to graduate from college instead of flunking out, failing myself and my parents, and messing up my life. By deciding to change my mindset, setting a goal, and making that extra effort, I became fully engaged in life. Eighteen months later, I had found myself, met my wife, and graduated from the Pennsylvania State University.

The decision to transform is key.

That decision to change came from deep dissatisfaction and pain within myself. It was ignited by asking these two questions:

What is the purpose of my life?

Why am I here?

Deciding to transform means discovering the purpose of your service and preparing yourself and your people to give that service more fully. That will bring your organization into the blossom of its beauty, magnificence, service, and profitability.

Accept the Need to Change

In 2003, I wrote my first book, *Deep Transitions: Jump Starting Your Business*. In it, I describe a learning model for deep transition or transformation. It starts with the idea of resistance to change, but then goes into the need to accept. Accept change and new values.

Again, values lead to beliefs; beliefs lead to feelings and mindset. Feelings and mindset lead to behaviors; behaviors lead to results. We can either resist or we can accept and allow things to be what they are. Certain factors are outside of our control. When the environment changes, the industry changes; regulations change, economics change. Then, your organization needs to change too. It must align its internal mechanisms with the external environment in order to achieve organizational effectiveness, or it's going to be left behind. Accept that change is the only constant in life and adapt, be agile. Those who learn the fastest win, and learning is synonymous with change. If we don't change our behaviors, it's questionable whether we have learned anything.

Also, change is synonymous with development and growth. Change is a natural part of life. Everything is changing; everything is growing. Either we're changing and growing, living on the growth edge, or we're dying in every moment. There's no in-between. Most of us don't like change because its uncomfortable, but I'm going to share with you a process that helps you recognize the mindset, attitudes, and goals that are keys to changing. When we can accept change, we can heal and grow. We can gather more of what we want in our business life as well as our personal life.

What's the opposite energy of acceptance?

Control.

Can you control the market?

You've got to change with the market. You've got to adapt, adjust, and be agile. Accepting the change and sending that acceptance energy out will bring you more things to accept and appreciate, and increase your service and the value of your bottom line.

Self-Reflection and Dialogue

Self-reflection and dialogue are two key processes in adult learning. My background and doctorate degree are in adult learning and transformational learning. With these two processes, we must allow ourselves to reflect. We offer our clients employee engagement surveys with fifty questions on culture, alignment, relationships, and accountability. These surveys are opportunities to give the client data that reflect on their current condition. Without self-reflection, it's hard to figure out where the gaps are and make the best decisions for progress.

Dialogue is the second process for learning, growth, development, and change. When I say *dialogue,* I don't mean just talking at someone. I mean seeking to understand other people's points of view. In Steven Covey's book, *The Seven Habits of Highly Effective People,* he writes, "Seek first to understand, then be understood."[7] That's a powerful idea. Most of us are not taught to participate in an effective dialogue. We're trained to want to tell everybody what's on our mind! To understand someone means you experience true communication, which is when both parties share the same meaning.

When I say *reflect,* I mean ask yourself questions, such as:

- *What am I doing?*
- *How am I doing it?*
- *Why am I doing it?*
- *Is it working?*

Then dialogue to understand others' points of view. To dialogue requires asking questions and listening to comprehend the answers. Those two processes will help you learn. As you learn and grow, you will change and develop yourself, your teams, and your organizations.

Supportive Relationships

I don't know the source, but some years ago I heard, "The difference between where you are today and where you'll be five years from now is the people you associate with and the books that you read."

---

7   Covey, Stephen R. *The Seven Habits of Highly Effective People: Restoring the Character Ethic.* New York: Simon and Schuster, 1989.

To move from where we are to where we want to be, we need to develop supportive relationships to help us learn what we don't know and do what we haven't yet done. If we already knew everything, we'd already have what we wanted. If we didn't need some type of support—not just knowledge support, but energy and action support—we'd already be where we want to be. Relationships with mentors who have done what we want to do are vital.

In his book, Alan Deutschman poses a question: "Could you change when change matters most?"

He opens the first chapter with: "Change or die. What if you were given that choice?"[8]

If you didn't change, your time would end soon—a lot sooner than it would have had to.

Deutschman shows that 90 percent of people who experienced heart attacks will not change within three years, even though they've been advised by doctors. Only 10 percent of those patients will change.

Supporting relationships require us to *relate*. Quoting from *Change or Die*, "You form a new emotional relationship with a person or community that inspires and sustains hope." That's the first of three keys the author names as essential to creating lasting change.

---

8   Deutschman, Alan. *Change or Die: The Three Keys to Change at Work and in Life*. New York: Harper Collings, 2007. 1.

The second key is *repeat*. "The new relationship helps you learn, practice, and master the new habits and skills that you'll need."

The third key to change is *reframing*. "The new relationship helps you learn new ways of thinking about your situation and your life."

I would add that new relationships help create not just new ways of thinking, but new ways of feeling about your situation. Your feeling world is where the power lies to change and acquire everything you want.

Why? Because our emotions ignite mental activity that leads to a physical manifestation.

Everything we've learned and everything we've obtained results from some supportive relationship that we've had from our childhood up until the day we pass away.

It's not just technical knowledge. It's relationships—*quality* relationships. We enroll our customers in relationships. If we want to improve our engagement at work, we need to enroll our employees in positive relationships that help them grow and develop because they're the ones who complete the work, who bring us profit.

There's a direct link between customer loyalty and employee loyalty. Employee satisfaction drives customer satisfaction. In fact, employee engagement drives customer engagement— it's the relationships.

Most people have a good product. Most people have a good service.

What's going to separate you from the other business?

It's your ability to enroll people in supportive relationships. Be supportive, and the support will come back to you.

It seems to me that everything in life is about transformation. Transformation is growth. We can decide to live in the darkness of ignorance, ignoring the realities of our current situation. Or, we can decide to live in the light of guidance to grow to greater maturity. Life is growing or dying in every moment. We grow from stage to stage. We transform from stage to stage, and so does our business.

CHAPTER TWO

Collect Data and Diagnose the Condition

DATA-GATHERING TECHNIQUES

To make the best decisions, you need the best accurate information. You need data. Sometimes people in organizations think that they know what's going on, based on intuition and hunches. There are data in intuition; however, to be more precise and to be accurate, it's important to have techniques that allow you to get the most complete data. Inaccurate or partial data lead to inaccurate and incomplete decisions.

The academic term for combining information from different angles or sources is *triangulation.* They say there are two sides to every story, and then there's the truth. You want to gather the information from as many sides as possible to find the truth.

Data collection is necessary not only to make the best decisions and the best plans but also to take the best actions to achieve your goals. Therefore, data-gathering is the foundation for developing learning processes to improve teams and organizations. That's why data-gathering techniques are shared in this chapter.

Interviews

The process of interviewing starts with identifying the key players you want to interview. Quite often in an organization or a team, the people who are decision makers —leaders and managers—are the first to be interviewed to get their perspective. These key players can be a focus group too.

The second step of interviewing is thinking through the purpose of the interviews and developing the right questions.

What is the purpose of this data-gathering process?

What is the information that you want to gather?

The best questions focus on people's experiences. The questions should be open-ended, not closed-ended, questions. A closed-ended question leads to a yes-or-no answer, or some specific, factual piece of data or number. Open-ended questions are interpretive. They give people an opportunity to share their opinions and perspectives. That's what you want because the more people talk, the more information they give you, and the clearer the picture they paint for you.

You need to see that picture clearly to analyze accurately and make decisions about the company's direction.

In addition to providing information, interviews create buy-in. Everybody wants to be heard and attended to. Individual interviews and focus groups allow you to serve that purpose as well. Sometimes in interviews, if it's agreeable with the person, you can record with audio or video, and those recordings help you maintain accuracy. Some people may not want to be recorded. Of course, you must respect that as well.

Lastly, interviews bring about education. By asking people questions and listening to their answers, you'll gain qualitative data. The quality of people's perceptions and their experiences are quite valuable.

Observations

Use more than one method of data-gathering to acquire well-rounded information. Interviews are one method; observations are another. Be clear about what you're looking for in your observations. Try being a *fly on the wall*. Put yourself in a situation where you can observe people's behaviors and comments without interjecting. Take notes about what you see.

Stay open to whatever you see. Remember that, in the interviews and the observations, you need to take good notes about what you see and hear, so later you can analyze more thoroughly the data you've collected.

The bottom line is: be clear about what you want to know, and gather the data by using these two techniques as a start.

Employee Engagement Surveys

Surveys are another way of gathering data. Employee engagement surveys have a particular focus. The reason you want to conduct one is because it gives you a baseline of your current state.

You need to know:

- Your current state
- Your desired state
- The gap between the two

This is necessary to grow, transform, create super performance, and increase profitability in your business or in your life in general.

Your survey should be anonymous and computerized to give you a thorough statistical analysis. We use fifty questions under categories of culture, alignment, relationships, and execution.

When considering engagement surveys, you want to:

- Ask about the *culture*:

  Do people feel respected, empowered, and challenged?

- Gather information about *strategic alignments*:

  Are people clear about where the organization is going and what their role is?

- Examine *managerial relations*:

  What are the relationships between employees and their managers?

  Are there positive interpersonal relationships and cohesive teams?

- Explore *managerial execution*:

  Are expectations clear?

  Are people being held accountable for their responsibilities?

For survey questions dealing with establishing a *culture* of engagement, categories might be:

- Respect for Employees
- Respect for Management
- Trust
- Teamwork and Cooperation
- Fairness
- Accountability

Some of the categories under *strategic alignment* are:

- Communication
- Purpose and Direction
- Organizational Effectiveness
- Values

As far as *motivating and relating,* they include:

- Interpersonal Relationships
- Cohesiveness of the Teams

Lastly, for *managing execution,* you want to include questions about:

- Accountability
- Execution
- Purpose and Direction

Make sure to include statements for each category that will drill down into your current state. It's important to use a statistically sound data source that covers a gamut of things. You want to be able to filter the survey to your specific environment and your specific structure.

For some clients, their organizational structure includes an executive team, a senior management team, directors, managers, departments, sections, and divisions. A bank might have branches, vice presidents, officers, a CEO, a COO, and tellers. A school might have departments, teachers, counselors, and so on. I want to be able to filter results in the most usable way for my client's business. Also, I want filters to look at generations, genders, and tenure. Yes, you want to ask questions, but you also want to be able to customize and filter the responses by what's important to you and by the structure of your company.

When we brought the survey data back to the leader of one company, he was amazed by the amount of data and the different ways we could analyze it.

In fact, his response was something like: "I can see there's a lot of money we're not getting because the details of these data are showing pain points, issues, things we're doing very well, and categories for improvement. We can see very clearly how to grow from the analysis and the diagnosis."

To properly diagnose the health of your organization, you must explore with leaders, managers, and employees:

- Statements, questions, and data about whether they are feeling empowered, challenged, and respected

- Where the organization is going and how they fit in

- Interpersonal relationships and cohesiveness of the teams

- Expectations and accountability

A particular client was ecstatic about the data and the fullness of the extent of being able to track the outcomes and performance to different levels and departments.

Surveying is not a performance tool, per se, but clients tell me, *It verifies and confirms things that we knew were going on, whether it was positive or negative.*

With data in hand, you can make effective plans. Our clients have developed priority categories a year or two in advance based on the fullness of the data collected and analyzed. One client decided they wanted to focus on the following categories: teamwork and cooperation, communication, accountability, and organization effectiveness.

The Culture and Health of Your Organization

Culture is really the big issue now. When you hire people, they expect the culture to be a certain way. If it's not positive and not the way they expect it to be, they'll leave. This is particularly true of the prospective millennials and Generation X employees. You must collect accurate data in its fullness to diagnose the organizational health, and then create some plans or treatments to grow.

In my twenty-five years of experience working in large consulting organizations, small consulting organizations, educational institutions, and my own practice for thirteen years, employee engagement surveys as a needs-assessment tool are the greatest thing I've seen. They can be thorough, detailed, and customized to a particular situation.

I guess I'm old school. I used to do interviews and focus groups and craft assessment tools from nothing. I still do sometimes, but the employee engagement survey really takes it to another level. I'm grateful to have it as a tool to get the best picture and help clients in the best way. I've also been blessed with twenty-five years of experience in interpreting these kinds of data, creating solutions that hit the mark, and helping organizations become healthier.

Patrick Lencioni points out in his book, *The Advantage*, that we spend a lot of energy on strategy, finances, and technology. Of course, these things have their place. He writes that there are two requirements for success—organizations must be smart *and* healthy:

> Smart organizations are good at those classic fundamentals of business: subjects like strategy, marketing, finance, and technology. . . . But being smart is only half the equation. . . . The other half of the equation, the one that is largely neglected, is about being healthy. [Indicators of organizational health are] minimal politics, minimal confusion, high morale, high productivity, and low turnover.[9]

He starts this book with a statement I love and want to share with you:

> The single greatest advantage any company can achieve is organizational health. Yet, it is ignored by most

---

9   Lencioni, Patrick. *The Advantage*. San Francisco, CA: Jossey-Bass, 2012, 5.

leaders, even though it is simple, free, and available to anyone who wants it.[10]

Although we've been conditioned for all the smart stuff—the strategy, marketing, technology, and such—when we create better organizational health, we gain competitive advantage. If the organization is not healthy, people leave. We know how much it costs to replace them. Turnover is one of the biggest expenses in any company, costing up to twice the annual salary to replace them. Then you've lost whatever you've invested in them. It's gone out the door! The cost of toxicity, bad attitudes, and turnover is great.

Just like when you go to the doctor to seek help with your body, you need to gather data and do tests. Likewise, these data-gathering techniques are necessary so you can diagnose the condition and then create treatment to attain greater organizational health, super performance, and profitability.

QUANTITATIVE/QUALITATIVE ANALYSIS

It's important to obtain both quantitative data (numbers) as well as qualitative data (comments) because they give you a certain picture of performance. When you know how to analyze those data, you get a different picture. Between the two types, they create a balance, and that's why it is critical to do both.

---

10 —, *The Advantage.* San Francisco, CA: Jossey-Bass, 2012, 1.

The Likert Scale

Under each of the four categories of survey questions discussed earlier in this chapter, there may be three or four statements that participants respond to. In our surveys, we include a five-point Likert scale like the one below, and we provide places for narrative comments. This is the best of both worlds, quantitative and qualitative.

Your scale might look like this:

(1)	(2)	(3)	(4)	(5)
Strongly Disagree	Disagree	Neutral	Agree	Strongly Agree

Review Scores and Distribution Data

When the results of the survey are compiled, you will see scores for each question. You can see the five-point scale above goes from a 5, which represents *strongly agree,* through a 1, which represents *strongly disagree.* If the average score employees mark is a 4.5 for a particular question or statement, then that's super. However, if it's a 2.1 on a five-point scale, then that's an area of concern. It's an area where there's pain and frustration in your organization as a body.

Our survey results show a bar graph distribution chart that identifies how many people answered strongly agree, agree, neutral, disagree, and strongly disagree. When the distribution is spread out between four or five responses, that's an indication people are having different experiences and perceptions about that specific item. This can be a cause for concern about questions dealing with trust, communication, respect, accountability, and so on. The broad distribution can be a sign of frustration and pain that will require attention. This is especially true when the distribution is skewed toward disagree and strongly disagree.

Review All Comments

Comments are the qualitative data. People's statements and interpretations of open-ended questions are valuable.

For example, one person from the group of new employees commented: "If you speak up in this organization, you'll get black-balled."

That is a definite sign of disengagement. They were in the organization less than one year.

Where did they get that idea?

Probably from a disengaged employee who was sharing their venom. Misery loves company. That's a very negative comment for people who are new to a workplace!

You'd want to address this type of attitude. It would be a good idea to meet with all the new people in a town hall or focus group meeting. You could use a focus group to gather more data about people's experiences and create an opportunity to set the record straight.

Another reason to review comments is to identify signs of active engagement. People will make positive comments about the work environment and why they're committed to making extra effort. Often, statements from engaged employees will provide solutions to underlying problems within the culture and managerial relationships. You'll want to analyze both sides of engagement and give attention to what's needed.

We often think of development and growth as focusing on the things that aren't working well and trying to fix them. That's one strategy. However, another strategy for growth is to focus on your strengths, focus on the things that engage people. Overall, you want to balance both, correcting what disengages people—what causes them frustration and pain—as well as focusing on those things that create commitment and passion and inspire extra effort.

Identify Related Themes, Connections, and Disconnections

After we gather the data, we like to meet with the leaders and managers first to look for themes. There may be individuals, teams, levels, millennials, or whatever groups you're looking at that have consistently low distribution on communication, or purpose and direction, or teamwork and cooperation. When you discover a theme, investigate whether it is organization-wide. You're searching for factors that drive the company to the desired state, as well as things that might be hindering it.

The theme can be any category that needs to be worked on, whether it's empowerment, leadership, motivation, respect, trust, or values. Survey analysis allows you to find themes you want to work on and go deeper into the data to know exactly what your focus needs to be.

Here's an example of connections and disconnections. At one company we worked with, the executive team was the most engaged while managers were disengaged. That showed us there was a disconnect between the executives and the managers. That's a big deal because the leaders depend on managers to execute the strategies and get results.

If a company's managers and leaders are disconnected, what will the managers pass on to staff and to the teams who execute the plans?

Search for the disconnections and connections that influence whether people are close in their perspectives and their actions toward the objectives of the team and organization.

DIAGNOSE ORGANIZATIONAL HEALTH

Positive organizational health can be a major competitive advantage for you. It can decrease toxicity, create engagement, and develop super performance to increase productivity and profit. Using the metaphor of a physical body to determine your organizational health, you collect data and diagnose the current condition of all organs, systems, and such. The departments, levels, and other kinds of filters identified before are all parts of the body

Muhammad the Prophet said: "There is in the body a clump of flesh. If it becomes good, the whole body becomes good, and if it becomes bad, the whole body becomes bad. And indeed it is the heart."[11]

We know that heart disease is one of the big killers in America. It can also be a killer in the health of an organization.

What does heart have to do with an organization?

Everything. The heart is a pump that moves the blood throughout the body. Blood represents the essence of life and life-force in the body. The heart is the center of emotion, including affection, compassion, and understanding. It is a symbol for love. The heart is expressed in humility, sincerity, genuineness, and vulnerability.

Heart-centered leaders are concerned about the amount of impact they and their organizations have on others. They see love and results as two sides of the same hand. When we love what we do and with whom we do it, then we can produce extraordinary results.

---

11   *Sahih al-Bukhari*, Book 2, Hadith 49. Paraphrased.

Identify Ideal and Severe Health Issues

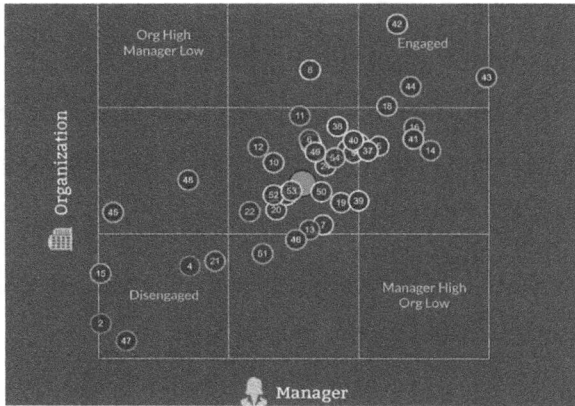

Once the results of the engagement survey are collected, it's time to analyze the data. We build a matrix derived from the algorithms of that engagement survey.

We have a matrix from the data, the algorithms of the particular engagement survey that gives us a chart, like a scatter gram.

The left side axis is organizational; in other words, it answers the questions:

Are people feeling respected and empowered?

Do they know where the organization is going and how they fit in?

That's one axis.

The other axis is the interpersonal, cohesive team relationships and accountability.

Picture a chart with three columns and three rows—nine boxes in all. The top right box would indicate high scores in those organizational factors—cultures, strategy, and high scores in the managerial factors—motivating and execution. That would be ideal health. Things are going well in the body. Then if the scores were high in the managerial, and middle in the organizational, the organization is not quite as healthy.

Your employees are the ones who bring in passion and give the extra effort. If they are part of a level, department, unit, team that scores high in organizational and managerial relationships, then that's ideal health. These are your engaged people.

If the team or department scores in the midrange on culture, alignment, relationships, and accountability, then they are not engaged. There's some dis-ease there. Those people are most likely going to be doing the minimum amount of work to get by—just enough to keep their jobs. They're on automatic pilot—nothing more and nothing less.

When the scores are lower in culture, alignment, relationships, and accountability, then those numbers represent actively disengaged employees who are frustrated and in pain. They're going to spread that negative energy. That's where the toxicity is, and that's where the severe dis-ease is. If you had that in your physical body, we would call it *cancer*. Some cancers you can't find without certain tests because they may not be obvious. This is what I mean when talking about ideal health versus severe health. You can see it in the output of the survey data.

Do you want to know how healthy you are?

Do you want to know how healthy your organization is?

If the answer is yes, why is that important, and what are you going to do with that information?

If you go to the doctor and they tell you that you've got a severe disease—a terminal disease—more than likely you're going to do something about that. When you go to the doctor and you get a clean bill of health, and you're doing well, you want to continue to do the good things that put you in that state. This is why identifying ideal and severe health issues is important.

Establish Priority Categories

Simply, you need to set priorities and goals at any given space and time. The markets are changing, legislation is changing, and economics are changing. These are the environments that businesses exist in. You want to align with that environment. You also need to cultivate alignment within your organization, in terms of your structure, strategy, technology, culture, people-development processes, and measurement systems.

When you're diagnosing the organizational health from the data, you want to establish your priorities for that particular time—for that year, or for the next couple of years—all focusing on improvement. Again, your priorities could be addressing areas of communication, teamwork and cooperation, accountability, or even organizational effectiveness.

After identifying categories for integrating into better health, you'll want to decide on goals and plans of action.

How are you going to treat those priorities and treat the condition in order to be healthier?

Share Findings and Conclusions

Once you decide your priorities for improving the organizational health, performance, productivity, and profitability, you've got to share that information with everybody. Every person, from the CEO, executive team, senior managers, and the managers, wants to know. Report to everyone so they can see the picture and be on the same page. We often hold company-wide meetings in order to share the findings of the survey.

Why?

Because people have invested their ten minutes to complete the survey and write their comments, and they want to know what came out of it. They also what to know what you're going to do about it.

Take this opportunity to share:

- What you found
- What you see
- What conclusions may be drawn
- The treatment plan that you'll execute

Share this information with everybody in the workforce, broadly at first.

Second, drive that same information down into the specific teams, so that each team sees where they are in relation to everybody else, and then they can begin to talk about what they're going to do in order to improve the work environment, their collaboration, and the support they need from the manager and the organization to become more engaged and more profitable.

To make progress in your company, you're dependent on the workforce in the field to execute the improvements. They will need your support. The best way to get people involved and to achieve buy-in is to invite them into the conversation as early as possible.

Once you've done your diagnosis and developed with your treatment plan, then share that with the rest of the body, the workforce, to engage them in the steps that will move you forward. Don't stop with one sharing. Communicate often through emails, activities, meetings, and so on. Remember there are values and belief systems that must be shifted, continually promoted, and demonstrated in behaviors to make a transformational shift.

The last step after you do the survey is to conduct a second survey. You could do a survey six months and twelve months after implementing the treatment plan. If you have a condition with your physical body, you're going to go back to the doctor to see how the treatment is working. The second survey will measure progress and identify areas for adjustments.

You can identify how far a unit, level, or whoever has moved from one year to the next. There will be positive trends as well as negative trends. Then, you start the process over again. Another survey, another analysis, another diagnosis, feeding that data back to the leaders—to the staff, determining the priorities for improvement, developing a treatment plan, implementing the treatment plan, and monitoring progress.

In one case, we saw significant increases in their overall engagement score and the percentage of engaged employees by 266 percent while decreasing the percentage of disengaged employees by 48 percent.

The culture almost doubled in terms of its number (from 22 to 40), and the execution and accountability went up by 27 points (38 to 65), which was a *huge* improvement.

Relationships went up by 22 points (43 to 63). Also, they increased their operating revenue year-over-year by $11 million. This was very gratifying for the client who worked hard to achieve these results in the first year. Afterward, we developed a second treatment plan to deepen the ownership of engagement at the management and team levels.

We're really excited about what we're able to do with our clients and the progress they're making.

CHAPTER THREE

Prescribe a Treatment Plan

EXECUTIVE MENTORING FEEDBACK

After collecting and analyzing the data, you need to create some type of treatment in order to improve the organizational health. Mentoring executives and giving that feedback is important because it continues the process of buy-in from the leaders of the organization. Of course, the executives are driving everything, so we want them on board. We want to cooperate, collaborate, and make sure that we are moving together with the executives in the process.

Share Specific Data With Executives, Senior Managers, and Managers

First, we set up a meeting to share data with the HR director, then the CEO. We go in with the *dashboard,* our way of organizing all the data from the survey. We want to start by examining the overall picture of the data.

It identifies the overall engagement score for the company, based on percentages of people:

- Actively engaged (bringing passion, energy, commitment, extra effort, and innovation)

- Not engaged (checked out, doing mediocre work— just enough to keep their job)

- Actively disengaged (frustrated, unhappy, and sabotaging work of the engaged people).

We examine these data in relation to the percentages of people feeling respected, challenged, empowered, strategically aligned, and accountable within their teams. We look at the data on trust, teamwork, cooperation, accountability, purpose and direction, organizational effectiveness, and leadership, and also at the data regarding motivation, communication, and respect.

Next, the data are shared with the leadership team and senior managers in a separate meeting. Then, eventually, we share with the managers and staff so that everybody sees the full picture of organizational health in that moment.

That's the idea. The purpose is everybody having the same information. Most of the time, if people have the same information, they will usually come to the same or a similar conclusion. At this point, we want to get people to buy in, especially the people who are going to be driving this change in organizational health.

Priority Areas for Leadership

As we're sharing the data, we pay attention to categories, particularly those categories where there are strengths. For example, if scores are high around values and executive managers supporting the mission and ethical standards, then that's a positive. At the same time, if there are lower scores on teamwork, cooperation, and communication, then we want to pay attention. These are areas indicating pain.

The goal of this dialogue with the leadership team is to identify three or four top-priority categories as areas for designing a *treatment plan* to address the needs. It could be a decision to focus on teamwork and cooperation, communication, accountability, and organizational effectiveness. One organization we worked with named those priorities. Thereafter, we looked at data under each of the categories to determine what learning processes were required.

In another organization, the focus might be on values, trust, fairness, respect for employees, and respect for management. It depends on what the data tells us, where the pain is, as well as where the positive things are, so we can create strategies for growth. Some strategies are designed to relieve the pain, but you can also have a growth strategy that focuses on those positive elements. This approach allows you to play to the strengths of your organization. Ultimately, there could be opportunities where you'll focus on both; you're dealing with the pain points as well as the strengths to bring the organization to optimal health.

Write Clear Goals

The next step is to have an individual meeting with each leader to view their specific data. One of the filters is groups of people who are reporting to a certain senior manager. That gives us the data of a shared perspective. We can show each leader the picture from their direct reports. This shows them clearly their team's answers to the fifty questions.

The picture of their team's overall engagement score could show there were no people actively engaged—50 percent not engaged and 50 percent actively disengaged. That means half the team is doing mediocre work, making errors, and possibly wasting resources, and the other half is frustrated and in pain. Their culture of engagement score could be in the danger area. Maybe they have low scores for accountability. People are not achieving the goals and meeting expectations. The manager may have low scores for communicating well with the rest of the organization.

You can consult each of the four quadrants and see what their scores are for *culture of engagement;* again, people feeling empowered and challenged. We can see their scores on *strategic alignment.* We can see their scores on *motivating and relating.* They may have very good relationships with the manager, they may feel cohesive as a team, and they may be executing tasks and being accountable, but their culture and alignment scores could be low.

The low scores indicate where we need to help them identify what the specific priorities are for their team. Then we can come up with what areas and actions they need to take to address their specific challenges, and come up with specific and measurable goals of what they can do to improve engagement in their team.

We do that with all the units, all the sections, all the branches, the leaders, managers, and each one of those teams within the organization. We move from the executive, senior management level to the specific leaders who manage those teams so they know exactly where they are. We support them in creating the specific measurable goals and actions required to move forward to super performance and increasing profitability.

Our process involves communication, teamwork, and mentoring in groups as well as individually. We meet people where they are in stages. All this is an education process—reviewing the data, the diagnosis, the prescription and executing the treatment plan. People at all levels must decide to be held accountable to us and the process to support the solutions. Through the experiences of assessing, training, and advising as a trusted mentor to the executives, clients can eventually begin to mentor their own folks and drive growth processes throughout the entire organization.

DEVELOP ACTION-LEARNING INITIATIVES

A Super Performance Employee Engagement Program will show you what's required and which actions are appropriate to produce the desired results. As human beings, achieving change, growth, and development requires we learn how to deal with our belief systems, attitudes, and mindsets—how we think and feel habitually about things. That need is going to drive how we behave and the actions that we take, which lead to the results we want.

In the last section, we discussed how to lay the foundation by collecting the data, analyzing the data, diagnosing the situation, and naming priorities. In this section, we discuss how to take the appropriate actions to grow.

New Activities and Communication Plan

Everything from this point forward must be communicated. It must be communicated from the executives all the way through to the rest of the organization. One organization liked to use emails, so we supported the executive in crafting emails that he would send out to support employee engagement. Data came back that people wanted to see the CEO more, so the communication plan included activities like lunch with the CEO. He met with groups and continued to communicate about strategic objectives, ask questions, and listen to the employees about what was on their minds.

We've held all-hands meetings for some organizations, in which everybody in the organization meets together. We support them by communicating what the plans are for engagement programs, as well as tying them into the CEO's comments.

The communication plan involves any contact with employees and the CEO, the senior managers, and the managers. You start with the executive team because, again, folks are looking to the leaders and are going to respond to how the leaders show up for any learning or employee engagement activities.

Based on the priorities and goals of the executive team leaders, we prescribe activities that the executive team can use to communicate, even in their regular meetings or their side meetings with individuals. We want to drive those initiatives through repetition of the message; people talking about them, people engaged in the behaviors that are required to get the results we need. It could be written communication, it could be verbal communication, or it could be any interactions.

How are you communicating with folks?

What is your major way of communicating?

One initiative of the communication plan—in addition to meetings, emails, and activities like lunch with the CEO— might be to set up an engagement committee. Enroll some of the millennial employees to participate in the committee and create an engagement newsletter and awards program.

Develop Training Curriculum

Once we identify categories and priorities, we develop a customized training program for the managers and the staff. The purpose is to learn to address those problem categories and improve employee engagement. The learning objectives are designed to ignite super performance.

For most organizations we serve, an objective is to increase their teamwork and cooperation.

At the end of the training, they are able to:

- Increase their teamwork and cooperation
- Enhance the trust and alignment within the team for organizational effectiveness
- Increase the accountability for results
- Capitalize on unique individuals' communication strategies
- Maximize differences in learning the communication preferences
- Apply strategies to resolve conflict

In this training, we know there are different trust-building factors. Executives see things a certain way. In fact, there was a study by Edelman Trust Barometer in 2012. There were six different items. When executives ranked these six items, the one item, "Treats Employees Well," was sixth for them. Treating employees well was third for the employees. You can see that there was a disconnect between how executives viewed trust, and how employees viewed trust in terms of behaviors that were built. Executives ranked *higher quality products and services, listening to the customers, taking action toward the stress issues, ethical practices, and placing customers ahead of profits above treat employees well.*

But the employees ranked *higher quality products and services* first and *listening to the customers* second. Their third-ranking item was that they wanted to be treated well, which scored higher than the other actions. That kind of information is important. We went over the five dysfunctions of the team, and we also used a learning style instrument so people could understand their learning preferences, how they communicate, how they solve problems, and how they make decisions.

Learning Style Preferences

The learning styles instrument is a powerful because it can help define some of the issues around how we see and communicate with each other. It creates major breakthroughs. In one organization where we did this, they began to communicate with each other through those learning preferences because they had a basic understanding of which framework would be most effective.

There are four different preferences in the tools, but we all have one or two that we tend to use more often, more frequently, and effectively. The learning style preferences aren't really labels, because everybody has some aspect of all the tools of each preference. Once employees at the company mentioned above understood their preferences, their learning styles contributed to how they made decisions, how they solved problems, how they communicated, and how they worked in teams. They began to communicate with each applying those ideas.

Company-wide communication improved as they understood themselves and each other. The survey tool explained the experiences they were already having. It provided them a framework and a common language from which to communicate with each other. They had a lot of fun understanding and explaining the interactions they were having.

This is just some of what comes out of a curriculum we design for a company. We train all the managers and all the staff so everybody has the same framework from which to work more closely and cooperatively with each other. Even while identifying strengths, we also want to help people identify their *least* preferences because those are the places that may be full of conflict for them. We also explore missed opportunities and miscommunication. We did multiple exercises, and employees walked away with tools and a chance to practice their skills to communicate better, to work better as a team, to cooperate with each other, and to be held accountable.

Implement the Happiness Campaign

The Happiness Campaign is an eight-week program designed to help individuals and teams—the whole organization—to move out of these negative energies of disengagement into energies of engagement and super performance on the positive side.

The campaign comes from some work I did researching participants in training programs.

The two research questions were:

1. When people act out of their ego, what do they do?
2. When people act out of their spirit, what do you see?

I collected data for three years, analyzed it, and wrote a book, *25 Days to Living Your Happiness*, which is the basis of this campaign. The ego's, or dis-eased ego's (as I call it) energies are based in fear, doubt, and worry. They start with selfishness. The habitually selfish person becomes dominant and then isolates themselves.

There are twenty-five different elements of this dis-eased ego energy that become worse from selfishness, into victim mentality, feeling powerless, dissatisfaction, and devaluation. Frustration is a common element in many individuals and teams. In fact, the disengaged people are usually involved in these types of energies—negative energies like frustration, punishment, judgment, and pain.

The Happiness Campaign looks at what type of energy individuals arrive with: Are they negative energies? Or are they the contrasting, opposite energies, the spirit energies based in love?

For example, instead of selfishness, being selfless makes a huge difference in developing relationships. Instead of dominating, move to the energies of communication where you're asking about other people's needs and serving those needs in order to connect.

- Instead of feeling like a victim, how about taking responsibility?
- Instead of trying to control, accept.
- Instead of punishment, try forgiveness.
- Instead of judging, be merciful.

The program begins with each person completing an individual happiness quiz. This self-assessment tool provides baseline data on the types of energies a person is using that contribute to their happiness and engagement or keep them stuck in fear and self-doubt. We set up a private Facebook group for ongoing interactions and questions. Then we facilitate eight weekly assignments and conference calls. Every week, participants are assigned certain chapters to read and exercises to do. The daily readings and assignments take about ten minutes to complete. They read three or four pages on the contrasting energies and then write an affirmation fifteen times to anchor it into the subconscious. Then they do an exercise to ground them in the positive energy for that day.

The outcome is more positivity within oneself and between each other. This activity changes the culture as individuals are seeking to make each other's work easier through better service and communication. Imagine what that will do for your employees' and customers' experiences. The premise of the activities is that as people feel better, they will do better and achieve better results. The weekly calls provide the opportunity to find answers to questions and create dialogue through sharing their experiences.

The evidence is clear that The Happiness Campaign moves people's attitudes and behaviors from negativity into more positive energy. It eliminates some of the toxicity that leads to the expense of preventable errors, poor performance, and turnover.

Universal law states whatever energy you send out is going to come back to you like a boomerang. We are grateful to have this tool and the ability to share it to improve the health of organizations, beginning inside the hearts and minds of the people.

Unfortunately, not all individuals will do the readings, affirmations, and exercises. The disengaged people might not want to do the critical self-reflection and dialogue required to be more engaged and happier. They might not want to feel better because their habit is negativity.

In contrast, some departments have done the program as a team. One group met every day for fifteen minutes, read together, wrote the affirmations together, and then did the daily exercises. It created a stronger bond between them. I remember one of the women commented how it helped raise her consciousness. It's a beautiful thing.

Learning Requires Action

We prefer to learn in different ways and for multiple reasons. Some people like to learn so they can analyze and create models. Some people learn to solve problems. Some people learn so that they can have alternatives and options. Lastly, some people learn to take action. It seems to me the real purpose of learning is to take action. Educators would tell you that if the behavior doesn't change, if action isn't taken, it's questionable whether you learned anything. *Learning, development, growth,* and *change* are all synonyms. When we act on what we learn, then we can produce the results we really want. That's why developing action-learning initiatives is critical for organizational health, increasing productivity, super performance, and eventually the profitability of your company.

DESIGN TRAINING AND DEVELOPMENT PROCESSES AND CONTENT

To emphasize the importance of this section, I want to make a distinction between training and development. *Training* is when one teaches someone new knowledge or new skills. Just because you supply your employees knowledge and skills doesn't mean they're going to use them. *Development* is when one uses those skills and knowledge to experience progress.

We need training, but more importantly, we need development. The first step is to make an effort to learn with your current talents. That gives you skill. The second step is to make an effort applying the new skills. That develops the *grit* which will produce the achievement you desire. Making effort to use those skills is the development that will give you the achievement you want. A course of training that allows for time to practice and develop new skills needs to be designed. This section discusses how to follow a development process to its logical conclusion.

Learning Objectives That Align With Priority Categories

Choose the general learning objectives you want to pursue and move toward specific outcomes that you want from the learning. People should be able to develop new specific behaviors as a result of each of the modules within your training. You want this to be tied directly to the priority categories that came from the analysis, diagnosis, and the meetings with the leaders. It's just as simple as that. That way, everything tracks back to the survey, which is the foundational data for building super performance and profitability.

The objectives give you goals. Again, learning is tied to action, which is tied to behaviors, which are tied to attitudes. These objectives and outcomes are the goals which you desire to achieve through learning and development.

Customized Workbooks and Training Materials

For twenty-five years, I've had the honor and privilege of helping people learn through this type of work, as well as teaching graduate school courses. Every situation is different. Every individual has different preferences about how they like to learn. I'm not a believer of a cookie-cutter approach. I don't think that works—where you just take something off the shelf and *throw it* at someone. I want to tailor and customize what I'm delivering, so that I make sure that it hits the mark. I make sure that the individuals and teams are receiving exactly what they need for their specific condition.

We've been talking about the organization as a body and improving organizational health. When you go to a doctor with a skin condition, would they grab a solution to treat some other part of your body? It doesn't make sense. You need something that's customized for the particular condition you have. We write workbooks and create training materials that are designed to treat the specific condition of organizational health that's coming from your employee engagement data, priorities, and such. This is how we do it. I believe that's the best approach to make sure you achieve the results you desire.

Experiential Learning Tools

People learn in different ways. You want the training you offer to make sense and last. Not everyone learns best through lecture or question-and-answer sessions. For this reason, we use *experiential learning,* or learning by doing. Instead of giving people a book to learn from, we provide exercises so that people can experience absorbing the knowledge and practicing skills. When people have an opportunity to apply the learning in a real situation, or to try out a new skill, they usually have an easier time integrating new knowledge and will remember the information or process longer.

Another important factor in learning is repetition. A lecture may open the door to understanding a topic, but without repetition, most of us are not going to remember more than a small percentage of that content.

Educational theory states that if you acquire a piece of knowledge today, within twenty-four hours, you're lucky if you remember 50 percent of it. Two days from now, you're lucky if you remember 25 percent of it. And two weeks from now, you're lucky if you remember 2 percent from that great article you read this morning. But if you have experience with it, you review it, and you use repetition—go over it and practice that knowledge so that it becomes a skill—then you're going to remember up to 62 percent of it for fifteen years to life.

That's why when I ask you, "What's four times four, two times two, and five times five?" you know the answers instantly. You have memorized those facts, and you 've used them over and over again. But when I ask you, "What's 14 x 13?" You have the skills to do the multiplication, but you don't *know* it by heart. It's not etched in your subconscious mind like those other numbers, right?

Instead of giving people a book to learn from, we use experiential learning. We provide exercises so that people can experience absorbing the knowledge and practicing skills. One method we use is role-playing. Not everyone likes to learn by role-play, however, so we include a variety of activities, such as real-life scenarios, case studies, and problem-solving examples. Some people learn best by lecture, and question and answer, even analysis of case studies and problem-solving examples.

So, you'll want a variety of instructional methods that will meet people at their learning preferences. For example, the pro and con grid involves learners developing a list of advantages and disadvantages about a suitable issue, helping them to see a topic from different angles and to develop skills in analysis and evaluation. The fishbowl activity involves a pair or group sitting at the front of the classroom and openly discussing an assigned topic so the entire classroom can hear and provide feedback.

This relates back to a tool mentioned in the previous section. Case studies give people an opportunity to analyze, to bring their experience into the analysis of a situation, so that they can learn. You can create your own case studies. It's nice to create case studies from the experiences within the organization. They become the most relevant examples. You can gain some of the cases from the information discovered in your individual meetings with managers to help them develop their priorities, as well as meetings with executive teams and focus groups.

Using experiential learning tools brings the learning out of the head down into the heart. When our heart becomes involved and we're learning through our heart, it's going to create certain feelings that will drive what we do. Our mindset and heartset drive our behaviors, and our behaviors drive our results.

We must build in learning examples for people that come from their life experiences or help them deal with their life experiences. Those examples make the learning relevant for them today. They can learn today and use it tomorrow. Then, through consistent practice, the new behaviors can become a habit in weeks. As they become proficient using the skills, the effort will turn into the achievement that the individuals and the leaders of the organization desire. As the old saying goes: *experience is the best teacher!*

CHAPTER FOUR

Take the Medicine

SCHEDULE AND CONDUCT TRAINING AND DEVELOPMENT

At this point, we've done the analysis, diagnosed the situation, and developed a treatment plan. It's time to implement the plan. That treatment is going to come in some type of training and development activities. These two aspects become part of the treatment and the medicine to improve your organizational health. They should be scheduled with multiple teams at different times.

This plan *is* the medicine and the process for taking the medicine.

Collaboration With HR

Collaboration—and maybe I could even say *cooperation*—with the senior person in the Human Resources department is critical because as a consultant or facilitator, I'm there to make her job easier. An engagement program is going to come through HR, as we want to work hand-in-hand, step-by-step with the senior person. They are the *point person*. The program becomes part of their goals under the strategic plan for the organization. So, it's vital to them because their performance appraisal and bonuses will be tied to the progress of the engagement program.

I've always seen our role as one that makes life easier for the HR person and makes them look good. This cooperation and collaboration requires asking what's important to them every step of the way and what their needs and interests are at every step of the way. We want to communicate openly, so they're willing to share with us how things continue to shift and evolve. We want to continue to receive feedback, to diagnose, and to make necessary adjustments that ensure desired outcomes.

Mutual cooperation means helping each other achieve desired goals. I only win when the HR director wins. Fortunately, the relationships we share with our clients are highly collaborative and highly cooperative. That's really what makes *taking the medicine* work.

The role of HR director is vital because they're getting information from the president, COO, and all employees. I can't do it without them, and they can't do it without me. It's almost like a marriage—a business marriage. When communication flows regularly—weekly, if not more than that—then we all grow.

My goal is that nothing happens, not even one inch is moved, without collaboration and cooperation with the HR leader. It can become a mentoring relationship as well. My role is not just to come in, train, and develop everybody but also to be a trusted advisor to the senior HR person. This relationship requires a lot of listening, mentoring, and teaching. When we have that kind of cooperation, everybody wins and everything is successful.

Training and Development Materials

When we are communicating the results at company-wide meetings, we develop the presentation to be reviewed by the senior HR person first. The curriculum for the training and development activities and additional engagement initiatives are created in collaboration.

Obviously, everything must be perfect and accurate, and it must:

- Be relevant for the organization
- Help them solve the problems that create disengagement
- Support more active engagement where people are innovative, bringing passion and energy to the job

Every PowerPoint slide, every word, every activity, every exercise—whether it's role-playing, case studies, lectures, Q & A, skill practice activities—must all be developed and customized as the treatment plan. There's no cookie-cutter approach. Sure, there are other materials as part of our toolkit—maybe developed by someone else that we insert in our customized prescribed *medicine*—but ultimately, everything has got to be relevant for the client's needs and aspirations. We take the creative process of preparing the materials very seriously.

Deliver and Evaluate the Training

In a mid-sized organization, there are a lot of different teams, and each of them will need training that should be scheduled. For example, we usually start out training the senior leaders, the executive team, the senior management team, and the managers. Thereafter, we serve their teams. We also deliver to them follow-up actions so the solution, the medication, can begin to move throughout the body of the organization. It starts with the leaders in their position of influence, and then it cascades down into other levels so the same message is being communicated.

If we were all healthy and whole, we wouldn't need this type of intervention. In other words, if people were already completely engaged and able to super perform, then they wouldn't need me. Since they've hired me to serve them, I make sure to be engaged with them at every level and that the medicine is pure regarding language, vibration, principles, practices, and skill development.

That's what I'm hired to be and do. I'm mentoring executives and senior managers. I'm helping them grow, develop, and practice certain skills until they can become proficient. That's part of our role, responsibility, and obligation. Sometimes we deliver in training programs, sometimes in one-on-one mentoring and counseling, and sometimes a situation may arise and I need to be available for a single employee to help them work through a situation. All that is part of delivering the service of creating cultures of engagement and super performance.

To evaluate training or mentoring we ask the following questions:

1. What worked?
2. What didn't work?
3. What ideas are you taking away?
4. How will you use these ideas?
5. How will you benefit from the application?

This information helps the client review important learnings for application. Also, it helps us know where to make adjustments for future training. An evaluation can be used as another needs assessment to guide the next steps.

We seek to serve in a way that makes things easier for clients. By cooperating with each other, we become a powerful team. That's why all must practice the therapy!

PRACTICE THE THERAPY

This section is critical. I used to work with a person who had some type of illness, and she had to change her prescription for the medication, but she didn't take the medicine. She said she didn't even read the prescription! She didn't even read the instructions on the bottle of the medicine she needed to take. If we're going through this process of doing the assessments—conducting the survey to collect data, analyzing the data, forming the diagnosis, creating the treatment plan—then it doesn't make sense to not read the prescription and take the medicine because that's where the healing is going to begin!

The particular medicine, the therapy, is specifically designed for your organization, for your situation. That's why this is important. This is where the consistent action comes in.

Apply What You Learned

The rubber meets the road when you apply knowledge and skills. Individual, team, and organizational change can be difficult when people don't want to do what is required to grow. Employees can be stuck in the current patterns of culture in the organization. The only way to grow is to learn and apply new concepts, techniques, and behaviors.

Unfortunately, most people won't change until they experience enough discomfort, dissatisfaction, and pain. Then we're ready to do something about it. Part of our work is to help people do new things until they become proficient at them. We're always harping on application, and part of that application is modeling the practice of new knowledge and skills. The results come from behaviors and the *right* action.

In his book, *The Science of Getting Rich*, Wallace Wattles writes, "Getting rich is not from doing certain things, but it comes from doing things a certain way."[12]

We want to help people do things a certain way: with purpose, faith, gratitude, and consistency. When we do things a certain way, then we are guaranteed to succeed.

Communicate With Your People

We want our initiatives to flow from the senior leaders throughout the whole organization. As a leader, experiencing training and development, it's important to return to your people and share what you've learned because they're curious and want to know. Communicating to others gives you another opportunity to review what you've learned.

We learn through *spaced repetition*. The more you review materials or practice certain skills, the more proficient you become at it. Sharing the main ideas and skills you've learned that apply to your teams and communicating every step of

---

12   Wattles, Wallace D. *The Science of Getting Rich*. New York: Penguin Group, 2007.

the way is a powerful way to repeat what you've learned. Regardless of the circumstances, as you learn to engage more, you want to share and plant the metaphoric seeds that are going to grow in the hearts and minds of your team members.

Part of communication is asking them about what they are interested in—what's important for them—as well as communicating what's important to you. For example, we do an exercise focused on values. We start with senior leaders. We allow them to pick their top values and share them with each other in a training session. They practice listening and learning what's important to each of their colleagues. We found that when people allow themselves to be vulnerable and share, there's a connection that happens. There's a trust that deepens.

People may not want to be vulnerable, but in vulnerability, there is strength. When I'm vulnerable with you, then that invites you to be vulnerable with me. When people are vulnerable, we learn to trust them. Trust is the foundation for this growth that must occur. We're obliged to get through some conflict as we grow and change, especially initially, but we can't get through the conflict unless we have trust.

Vital to developing trust are:

- Communicating
- Inquiring
- Listening
- Sharing

Receiving feedback is all part of the process of developing trust. Communication is the vehicle for the process to engender trust. Sharing and caring: that is the way.

Stop, Start, and Continue

When we are making change, when we're learning, developing, and growing, the first requirement is that we stop patterns and habits that aren't working. It's only intelligent that when you're doing something that's not working, to stop doing it to bring about growth.

One person we've worked with, a vice-president, involved her company in engagement processes because the culture of the people working there was unhappy. The vice president did a survey in a group of forty people to discover why. Employees had been happier before, but now, all of a sudden, they were not happy.

What would make them happier in their experience?

They found out that people hated the work environment and felt they didn't get acknowledged. They used to have bonuses and special activities, but those things stopped. They didn't see the CEO enough, and there was no accountability. There were hard-working people, and others weren't working as hard. These became examples of things they had to *stop* doing in order to be healthier.

Then, there are things that you must *start* doing. To address the CEO not being visible, they developed an initiative for a monthly activity with the CEO, lunch or coffee, when anybody in the company could schedule a meeting with the CEO to discuss their concerns and to build a relationship. If there's no accountability, then you want to start to put processes and systems in place where people will be held accountable. If relationships and the team are not cohesive, then you want to start doing activities that will bring about more cohesiveness in the team. Those are interpersonal relationships, and it starts with the leaders and trickles throughout the organization.

So, you stop certain things, you start certain things, and then, make sure you continue doing what's working. The *magic* is in the follow-up and the follow-through. That's why we talk about *development* because it's a process as well. Stop, start, and continue. You continue to reassess, so that you can adjust and fine tune until people become strong in the new processes and in the new way of being at your company.

Disengagement is a dis-ease in the organization as a body. When you have some type of disease in the body, you want to stop doing certain things, and start doing others. Maybe you need to change your diet. Maybe you should start taking your medicine, or maybe you need to continue your medicine. Maybe it's exercise. Whatever the treatment is, it always comes down to stopping certain things, starting certain things, and continuing until you get the results— better health possibilities.

BEGIN THE HEALING

Understand that healing is a process. It has a beginning, a middle, and an ending, which leads to more strength. When you and your people put effort into learning, then skills will be developed. This is the first stage of healing. When consistent effort is made to use the new skills, the second stage of healing begins. Persistence and consistency lead to the third stage, which is achievement.

Measure Your Progress

We require measurement systems. There's an old saying: *Inspect what you expect.*

If you don't inspect what you expect to be done, it's hard to know if you're hitting the target, if you're really making any progress. Measurement systems reveal to you whether the initiatives are actually working.

There are short-term and long-term measurements. For your financial goals and other required activities, you can measure those on a weekly, monthly, or quarterly basis. That progress should be measured according to the engagement initiatives and how they are designed to get your desired results.

All the initiatives are more than knowledge and skill because you want to create an atmosphere like a family, where star performers are rewarded, acknowledged, and appreciated. You'll want to host get-togethers with employees, such as annual events where their families can be invited. You may consider recognizing your managers with special outings, such as fishing trips, golf trips, or certain types of things that can bring them closer together. Activities such as these, including retreats or making coaching available for people, are going to add to your progress.

At one company, they offered numerous types of these initiatives. When they started, people didn't like the environment. There was no accountability, and manager-employee relationships were poor. The culture was ill. At that time, they were generating $30 million in annual revenue. They began the processes of assessing, learning, developing, training, and coaching consistently. In four years, they grew to a $100 million company. They achieved significant progress because they changed the culture; the culture became more engaged. Relationships became better and more cooperative. Expectations became clearer, and employees were more accountable.

The bottom line is that people will be more and do more. Employees become more engaged when they know that their employer cares about them as an individual person. This is really where the healing begins: sharing and caring. Not caring about the employees as their positions, but as people. When people feel you really care about them, they will begin to care about the company, and begin to give more. That care will appear as you measure your progress on specific initiatives, and the metrics within those measurements will be positive over time. Growing from $30 million to $100 million in four years is excellent progress.

Wouldn't you agree?

You can measure the progress of whether people feel cared about because you see their attitude shift. As their attitudes shift, their behaviors will shift. They'll be more respectful. They'll be more appreciative. They will begin to behave with more kindness toward one another. You'll be able to see that in what people say, what they do, and how they treat each other. That will be the ignition for your progress.

Sense of Accomplisment

At every turn in this growth process there will be causes for celebration and to feel a sense of accomplishment. Each successful meeting, attitude, and behavior change is positively an accomplishment. The shift may start off slowly at first, but as you continue to build momentum, you'll see more achievements. Each success will inspire more accomplishments.

The feeling of achievement invites us to grow even more, to be, do, and have more. We need to shift out of our heads sometimes, and allow ourselves to feel in our hearts. We must be able to share those feelings with somebody. When people are making a conscious change, find them doing something good and celebrate it. When employees are demonstrating the required behaviors and accomplishing the desired results, help them feel good about all that.

The best leaders are those who show appreciation and thanks to their people for what they're accomplishing. They do this consistently with little things. You'd be surprised by how far a small, handwritten note with some chocolate candies in a little bag or a café gift card will go toward thanking your high-performing employees. These examples generate a sense of accomplishment. The better we feel, the better we do. The better we do, the more results we're going to get.

Our habits don't start with what we know; we don't always do what we know. Our habits start with how we feel. Our energy is in our emotions. That's where our power is, and that's what drives us to the behaviors that we do repetitively. They will be our habits. When we shift those habits, we also create more of the results we want.

Strengthen Engagement Through Consistent Action

I want to talk a little bit about strengthening engagement through consistent action. In order to heal, to become healthier, to reach the results we want, we must reach a point, a place of strength around the new environment, around new attitudes and behaviors, and this movement requires engagement.

In Chapter One, I shared the story of the mercy I experienced through being diagnosed with liver cancer. We talk about a body being sick, and remember, an organization is like a body. Before the transplant, they told me I would live for maybe eighteen months if I didn't do anything. The mercy is I was blessed to survive the transplant and live for eight years at the time of this writing.

In the treatment experience, I learned to be resilient. There were specific steps because I had to learn how to eat again, stand again, and walk again. Then, I had to take the prescription medication on a schedule every day. Initially, I took thirty-three pills a day. Persistence and consistency were required. We could say that, for an organization, the pills are the training and development exercises, the initiatives, and the mentoring sessions.

I also needed to rest. I had to do physical therapy, walk, and take action daily. I had weekly doctor's visits for labs and such. This could be challenging, especially those first three months. I had to have daily, weekly, and ninety-day goals and actions, until I could get back to work. Even still, it took me time to regain my strength. Likewise, individuals and teams will require daily, weekly, and ninety-day goals.

I also had helpers. I had a mentor, a coach. and a caregiver. My #1 supporter was my wife, Barbara Daaiyah. She was incredible; she nursed me, supported me, and gave me tough love when I needed it. I had doctors, nurses, and staff from Georgetown University Hospital. I received encouragement from family and friends. All this, again, was part of this process of gaining strength. This type of mentoring and coaching support system is required in a growing organization too.

All this changed me inside. Internally, I developed an attitude of gratitude for this mercy. I took baby steps every day. I didn't measure my progress daily; I measured it weekly and monthly. I had to accept setbacks and adjust from time to time.

Thankfully, I did gain my strength eventually. After a couple of years of this process, I was back to health, even better than before. I grew in business and life and was able to make greater contributions through our organization. In fact, this whole engagement service that we are involved in now came on the heels of these experiences and challenges.

How can the experience with healing my body relate to healing and strengthening your organization as a body?

Gaining better organization health will require resilience, taking the prescribed *medicine,* engaging mentors, and developing attitudes of gratitude.

This is how I have developed the understanding and leadership for creating cultures of engagement and super performance in organizations. I am in an excellent position to help others heal and create cultures of engagement because I experienced that in my physical body, with my family, and with my team of doctors, nurses, family, and friends.

That's the approach we take in our work with organizations, as well as executive mentoring. We're part of the team to help your organization become healthier, so we can enjoy the benefits of a productive and profitable life. I got a second chance at life, and I'm using it to do the work I'm most passionate about.

When we're ill with disease, the most important thing is to believe that we can be healed, that we can be cured. We may not know all the details about how, but if we trust and believe that we can have better health, and we're willing to do what's required, then in fact, we will have better health. We will integrate and achieve better health, better business, and better lives. We just need to take the medicine and go through the process.

CHAPTER FIVE

Monitor and Adjust to Sustain Engagement

FOLLOW-UP TESTING

When you're improving a health process, it's important to have follow-up testing. In the last chapter, I talked about my liver transplant. I went in for follow-up testing on a regular basis; more testing earlier on. The closer to the surgery, the more testing they did. Eventually, I was at the point of weekly, monthly, and quarterly testing to monitor the status of my recovery.

That's the only way you can measure progress and make sure you're not going backward. The magic is in the follow-up and follow-through. That's why this section is vital.

Repeat the Engagement Survey

After you've done your initiatives, you'll want to repeat the engagement survey. You measure the same filters—the levels, departments, sections, those who report to certain individuals, gender, whatever the filters are.

Once you've measured more than once, you can observe *trend lines*. We measure where a particular unit was last year and compare it to where they are this year. You see if there's a significant improvement. The results are compiled into a graph that shows improvement as green lines moving up toward the *ideal box,* the engaged box, of high organizational culture and alignment, and high managerial relationships and accountability.

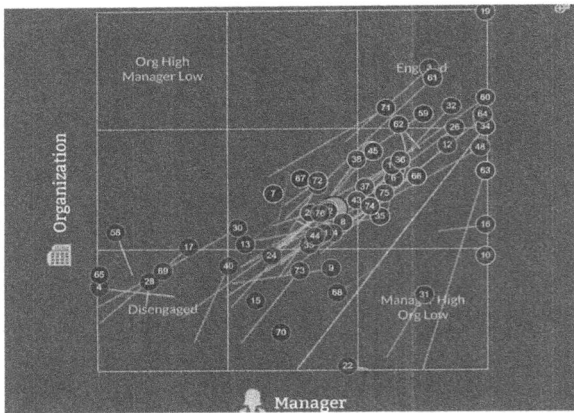

In one particular company, we were able to decrease the number of people who were in the disengaged boxes—those who were feeling disrespected, not strategically aligned, unaccountable for results, and described poor relationships with the managers—by 48 percent. We also increased, by

266 percent, the number of people in the engaged boxes who were feeling more valued and empowered and who were clearly aligned with their roles and responsibilities.

Follow-up testing gives us the current picture, and it shows the benefit of effort from the activities to treat the health of the organization.

Those results just mentioned showed the following improvements:

- Culture improved by 18 points
- Strategic alignment by 11 points
- Managerial relationships by 22 points
- Accountability by 27 points

The follow-up testing allows you to see exactly how engagement and performance have improved.

While keeping the same filters makes it possible to observe trend lines, you may want to add new filters to see what's been learned since the year before. Because you're doing the follow-up, you have the opportunity to make those adjustments and decide where you want more detailed data that you didn't get the previous year in your survey.

Diagnose Organizational Health Again

We want to maintain your super performance through engagement. We follow the same process as before. We look at the details, but now we have a slightly different picture of the decrease of those in the disengaged boxes, and the increase of those who are more engaged. So, you have a different diagnosis. In some cases, we have found that we've gotten rid of some of the severe illnesses and were left with two or three different units that were still disengaged, as compared with dozens before that.

We help you determine where the priorities are based on the new data—which units need more attention, which managers need more attention—and then we determine how to leverage the positive trends of those who increased significantly. We've had some units increase their overall engagement score by 35 to 50 points. We diagnose how to leverage the things that individuals are doing to make significant improvements. Then we disseminate that information, and the processes reach throughout the organization.

The diagnosis helps you answer these questions:

- What training is needed?
- Who needs to be trained and developed further?
- What types of mentoring are needed?
- Who needs the mentoring?

That leads us again to additional interventions for more progress during the next year.

We spend so much time in strategy, technology, finance, and technical areas, but it's important to remember that the healthier you are as an organization—the healthier the individuals and the teams are—the better you'll be able to execute your strategic plans and get the results you want. Organizational health is a competitive advantage. It's difficult to perform and sustain performance at maximum level. That is why we diagnose the organizational health again.

A New Treatment Plan

You want to increase the continuity of progress from one year to the next, and so on. You want to resolve any gaps between employees. Let's say we see in the results from the second survey that the executive team is more engaged, for instance, and we see that the managers are less engaged than they were the previous year. This means the gap between the engagement of the executives and engagement of the managers has widened in the second year. We want to resolve that gap. We create a treatment for the managers and a treatment to lessen that gap.

We prescribe executive mentoring as well as developmental activities for the managers, and we mentor and train employees so that they can be more fully aligned. If strategic alignment was your area of least progress from year to year, then you might decide to focus on that, and develop treatment activities, and initiatives to address that organizational factor.

Remember to build systems of accountability to accelerate the results. Exercises can drive the responsibility and ownership of engagement down to the managers and teams. And of course, conduct periodic assessment, monthly and quarterly, to monitor and sustain this higher performance.

Follow-up testing gives you a clearer picture of where you are and what the results of your efforts have been. It guides the prescription of a new treatment plan to gain even greater organizational health, productivity, and profitability.

EMPOWER MANAGERS TO TAKE OWNERSHIP OF ENGAGEMENT

Clearly, the president, CEO, COO, HR director, and executive team members should model the desired improvements that create engagement and organizational health. Yet, it becomes super-important that the senior managers and the managers become empowered to take the responsibility for engagement within their units. They may have to learn how to support their people even more to take the ownership of driving the engagement.

Ownership means managers helping make other people's work easier for them, and creating that type of empowerment among the staff members, so that everybody seeks to make everybody else's tasks easier. As people are serving each other, there's a feeling of empowerment and respect that moves throughout the teams and organization. It becomes a powerful, special experience.

Mentoring for Executives and Managers

Executives and managers may need assistance and support to execute their initiatives and responsibilities so that they may raise results, particularly if units' performance and engagement has gone down. If they knew how to raise the results, raise the profitability and productivity, then they would have already done it. Mentoring becomes a way to support them in their specific needs related to their responsibilities and outcomes for the company.

Mentoring can be one-on-one. It can be weekly or bi-weekly. The executives and managers are driving the agenda. Business is fluid, and change is constant, so we work one-on-one with executives and managers to help them develop new skills. We bring our twenty-five years of experience in learning, development, change, and growth with individuals, teams, and organizations, in a one-on-one situation with executives and managers, to respond to their specific needs and interests.

Connect Individual and Organizational Values

There's a diagram that we use, a triangle, and at the base of the triangle are *values and principles*. The next tier up from the values is *beliefs*. The values are the foundation, and then the beliefs come from there. Then from the beliefs, you have *attitudes and mindset*. The next level is *behaviors*, and the top level is *results*.

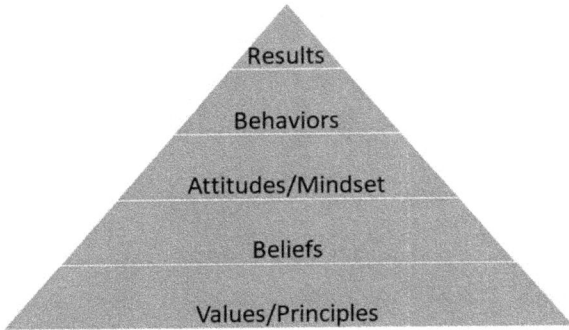

Values are the foundation. We work with leaders and people throughout the organization to clarify their individual values. We ask everyone to choose their top five or ten personal individual values from a list we've provided. They write those down and draw a picture that represents their values and what's important to them. Everybody is encouraged to share. When they share, they become vulnerable. As discussed in Chapter Four, shared vulnerability is one of the building blocks of trust. It's a powerful experience when people are sharing what's important to them, and others are listening and learning what's important to their colleagues. We've witnessed major breakthroughs in trust during this part of the exercise.

Then, we place their individual values on a chart underneath the organization's values. Everyone can see the chart and discern which principles are important to the individuals and how they match what's important to the company. Then at the end of the exercise, we facilitate the group coming to an agreement to commit to demonstrate those values. Cooperation is a major principle, working together and helping each other.

Once we do the exercise with executives and senior managers, we task the managers to conduct a similar exercise with their teams, so that they listen to what's important to the individual team members. It brings about more respect and a deeper sense of caring for each person as an individual. People connect individual to individual, as well as connecting individual values and principles to the company values. Again, it leads to more empowerment.

Team Engagement Accountability

In order to drive the ownership down to the teams, we do an exercise to bring in accountability. We start off comparing the *What Is* zone, or the comfort zone of the status quo— your current situation—and share and contrast that with the type of context and environment you *want* to work in. The *sacred context,* I call it. Most of us want more fulfillment, more respect, more love, and more communication. We want nonjudgment in our work environments, more peace, appreciation, kindness, generosity, gratitude, vulnerability, integrity, and such. Many other principles are part of this sacred context. We ask team members to create four or five statements of what they are willing to be and do to maintain this sacred context.

In one group, they agreed to: *I am willing to learn, change, grow, and develop. I will be vulnerable. I will communicate openly, and I will be truthful in love.*

After they form the agreements, we show them their specific employee engagement results of what percentage of employees in their particular team are engaged. Again, those employees will bring passion, energy, commitment, and extra effort.

We then show them the percentage of people on their team who are not engaged, who are doing mediocre work, settling, and who are doing just enough to keep from being fired.

Next, we show them the percentage of those employees within their team who are disengaged or frustrated and in pain. We show them how their results compare with every other unit within the organization, so they see how they're stacking up against their peers.

After viewing the results, ask:

- In what ways would you like to improve the work environment?

- What are you as an individual willing to do to improve the workplace?

- What support do you need from your manager or from the organization to actualize these improvements?

If you do this throughout all the units, folks will become more accountable. They will improve their processes, they will improve their relationships, and they will become more accountable to achieve those strategic objectives that you ask.

People feel more empowered when they can buy in to what you want to do. People buy in when they perceive that they have a voice, an expression, and their expression is being respected. These exercises are designed to give people an opportunity to express themselves, to be listened to, to be understood. That, in and of itself, ignites a process of people becoming more engaged, more empowered, and more respected. It builds trust and more engagement.

CONNECT ENGAGEMENT WITH PERFORMANCE OF BUSINESS METRICS

Engagement includes passion, commitment, extra effort, and bringing positive energy and solutions to work. Engagement becomes alive and real when it's tied to things that are measured. Sometimes, engagement is understood as something separate, until we make this type of connection. Then, it becomes more concrete because ultimately their appraisals are going to be tied to how well they meet the metrics and engagement support.

Link Engagement Results to Business Metrics

Let's say the organization is a bank, and one of the metrics you measure are bank deposits. You see from the engagement survey results that a unit involved with deposits is low in accountability or low in teamwork and cooperation. When you review the deposit metrics, you may want to look at some of the processes that you're using to improve the teamwork and cooperation.

If the team is not working cooperatively, how can you improve the process?

In a school, student performance and achievement are measured. If the students aren't engaged, then they're not going to perform well. That becomes a link to the metrics, but you also look at faculty engagement. Faculty engagement is going to drive student engagement, which is going to drive achievement. Just like employee satisfaction and loyalty is going to drive customer satisfaction and loyalty, which is going to drive the results and the bottom line of the business.

Tie engagement to whatever metrics you measure.

Are people willing to refer their family and friends to your business?

It's called a *net promoter score.*

When the percentage of promoters of your business is greater than the percentage of distractors, then your net promoter score will be high. Obviously, that's going to help your bottom line, because 83 percent of business comes from referrals. I don't know where I read that statistic, but it's a pretty standard idea. We want to link our engagement results from those elements that need improvements, as well as those that are going well, to the specific things you're measuring in your business.

Revise Systems, Processes, and Procedures

All that we've done up until this point—the survey, the analysis, the diagnosis, the treatment plan, the mentoring, the training, the Happiness Campaign, the accountability activities, the values—is driving us. Connecting these engagements to the metrics is driving us to review systems, processes, and procedures. Having built enough trust, having improved the health of the organization, you can involve people in revising those processes, procedures, and systems from the beginning. They're going to do much better executing the plans and initiatives because they've had a say in it, they've bought into it, they own it, and they take full responsibility.

As we improve our processes and systems and become more efficient and effective, we begin to see acceleration in productivity and profitability. One of the companies that we worked with improved their year over year gross revenues by $11 million. We all want to increase revenues, but the inner work within employees must be done before seeing the outer monetary results. It's like the inner emotional, attitudinal, mindset improvements are the *roots* of the organizational tree. The mental aspects of vision, mission, strategy, and structure are like the *trunk* of the tree. The profits are like the leaves or *fruits* of the tree. In this analogy: *the roots create the fruits.*

Follow-Up and Follow-Through

My mentor says that the money is in the follow-up. I would add that the money is also in the follow-through. As we've made these adjustments—we've taken our medicine, and we've gone through the process of recovery and becoming healthier—we need to follow up and hold follow-through meetings. We must *inspect what we expect,* and that will only occur by having consistent meetings. You might opt for morning or weekly huddles.

It's a good idea to include engagement in the discussions during your daily, weekly, and monthly meetings. This will increase accountability and make sure people are supported as they follow through on what they've agreed to do. The more you serve your people, the more your people will serve you and the organization. The increased accountability, service, and communication will come together to lessen the expense of preventable errors and turnover. It will also increase productivity, customer ratings, and profits.

Stay the course is another catch phrase. If you've done all this work, made plans, adjustments, and stayed the course, then follow the logic to its conclusion. Everybody will win!

Conclusion

I want to leave you with something that's relevant for your reality. I would ask you to look for what applies to you, at whatever stage you're involved in, and gain closure by using some of the techniques and exercises in the book to improve your team and workplace culture.

You can transform your reality, regardless of your history or whatever frustrations and pains might be visible.

You can diagnose, treat, and improve your organizational health.

It takes work, and in some situations, it's not easy, particularly if there's a lot of disengagement and illness. But the process works. I want to reassure you the process will work for you, so I'd like to leave you with that reassurance. If you follow what's in the book, follow the process, you will reach good results that will improve performance and improve profitability. Cultivate that energy of hopefulness, knowing the organization is not powerless. The organization is not powerless. With the energy of hopefulness, things can and will get better. It shifts the energy in a positive direction. Take the positive approach, and you'll get positive results.

Now that you've read this once, I encourage you to read it again. The reason for the second reading is *spaced repetition*. The more times we review something, the more likely we are to retain it, and the more likely we're able to understand it and to use it at its best application. Aside from just reading it, I encourage you to study it. Maybe in your second reading, study those sections that are most relevant to you. This process progresses stage by stage from identifying the need for change to doing what's required to grow.

Many organizations need change, but they're so stuck in their habits that they don't see the dis-ease. Or, they see it but they don't move on it. They're stuck in strategy, finance, and technology and tend to neglect their organizational health. First, identify that there's a need for some improvement of health, and then collect the data, diagnose, create a treatment plan, and execute that treatment plan. Assess again and make adjustments. You might need to focus more in depth in one of these stages. If that is the case, I encourage you to do that.

Use this book and trust the process. Change can be daunting, time-consuming, and costly in energy and money. But disengagement, toxicity, and turnover is much more expensive and destructive because it leads to organizational deterioration, cultural deterioration, managerial relationship deterioration, misalignment, and lack of accountability, which all lead to organizational death. Find something to use, take baby steps consistently over time, and trust that it will work for you.

You can do this! If you are serious and you persist, you can make it work for you. You would not have been guided to read this book if you hadn't had the capacity and the power to make this work for you. Trust that.

Next Steps

Please contact me with any questions. Contact me to be an ear, if you have a thought about a direction you'd like to take, or questions, or if you just need a sounding board for ideas about improving engagement. I'm here to serve, and I'd be happy to receive and respond to your questions.

Send me any comments about the book that you have found to be helpful. That would be useful for me as we continue this journey. Any testimonials are great. Also, contact me to explore how we might be able to help you at whatever stage of your transformation and growth process, whether you are assessing, looking for good advice and a trusted advisor, or training and developing your people so you can improve processes in your organization.

You can take any of these steps and use what's relevant for you, but the main thing is to *do something*. Nothing's going to happen if you don't act. Instead of looking at it as a big mountain to climb, I encourage you to explore where you can take baby steps. If you take baby steps consistently, that will add up to a mountain of achievement. Take action, take consistent action, baby steps at a time. That's how we grow and improve.

Please share this book with friends. Encourage your friends, leaders, and managers to get their own copy of the book and to read it, or give the book as a gift to people you think would benefit. Have them contact me if they think I can be of any assistance. You'll get the benefit of doing some good for someone by gifting it to them, and they will thank you for it, especially if they are having some pain and frustration and they're ready to do something about it.

People who are closed-minded, don't want to grow, or have a lot of fears, self-consciousness, or arrogance probably wouldn't want this book, so save your money. But if you feel that they're open-minded and ready to grow, it could be a good gift for them. Leaders are readers. We've got to read in order to be on the cutting edge of growth. We've got to be doing something with ourselves—our minds, hearts, attitudes, behaviors, and skills. This being and doing is engagement and is a process to creating super performance and profitability.

You can contact me at drz@universalselfleadership.com or for additional resources visit LinkedIn at linkedin.com/in/dr-zayd-abdul-karim-386a6031/ or our website at universalselfleadership.com.

About the Author

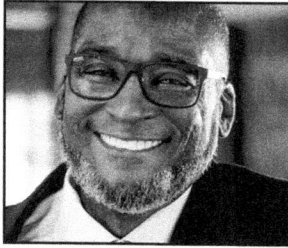

Dr. Zayd Abdul-Karim is a leader in transformational learning and self-leadership. Affectionately called "Dr. Z," he is a keynote speaker, mentor, and professional trainer. Zayd is a catalyst for growth and inner peace and serves to help individuals, teams, and organizations transform their lives and businesses through more engagement and super performance, which means living with more passion, commitment, and extra effort.

Dr. Z is the Founder and Chief Learning Officer of Universal Self-Leadership Institute (U.S.L.I.), a world-class provider of employee engagement, super performance, and customized leadership development services. He finds unique solutions to help individuals and teams deal with their dysfunctions that cause mental, physical, and emotional stress, which lowers productivity and profitability. His messages of positivity, happiness, peace of mind, and self-leadership inspire individuals to feel better, do better, and increase their lives and businesses. His tools and techniques are empowering and support a growth mindset.